weblinks

You don't need a computer to use this book. But, for readers who do have access to the Internet, the book provides links to recommended websites which offer additional information and resources on the subject.

You will find weblinks boxes like this on some pages of the book.

weblinks

For more information about globalisation, go to www.waylinks.co.uk/series/21debates/globalisation

waylinks.co.uk

To help you find the recommended websites easily and quickly, weblinks are provided on our own website, **waylinks.co.uk.** These take you straight to the relevant websites and save you typing in the Internet address yourself.

Internet safety

↗ Never give out personal details, which include: your name, address, school, telephone number, email address, password and mobile number.

↗ Do not respond to messages which make you feel uncomfortable – tell an adult.

↗ Do not arrange to meet in person someone you have met on the Internet.

↗ Never send your picture or anything else to an online friend without a parent's or teacher's permission.

↗ If you see anything that worries you, tell an adult.

A note to adults
Internet use by children should be supervised. We recommend that you install filtering software which blocks unsuitable material.

Website content

The weblinks for this book are checked and updated regularly. However, because of the nature of the Internet, the content of a website may change at any time, or a website may close down without notice. While the Publishers regret any inconvenience this may cause readers, they cannot be responsible for the content of any website other than their own.

HODDER
Wayland

21ST CENTURY DEBATES

GLOBALISATION
THE IMPACT ON OUR LIVES

ROB BOWDEN

HODDER
Wayland

an imprint of Hodder Children's Books

21st Century Debates Series

Genetics • Surveillance • Internet • Media • Artificial Intelligence • Climate Change • Energy • Rainforests • Waste, Recycling and Reuse • Endangered Species • Air Pollution • An Overcrowded World? • Food Supply • Water Supply • World Health • Global Debt • New Religious Movements • The Drugs Trade • Terrorism • Racism • Violence in Society • Tourism • Transportation

Produced for Hodder Wayland by White-Thomson Publishing Ltd, 2/3 St Andrew's Place, Lewes, East Sussex BN7 1UP

© 2003 White-Thomson Publishing Ltd

Published in Great Britain in 2003 by Hodder Wayland, an imprint of Hodder Children's Books.

Project editor: Kelly Davis
Commissioning editor: Steve White-Thomson
Proofreader: David C. Sills, Proof Positive Reading Service
Series and book design: Chris Halls, Mind's Eye Design
Picture research: Shelley Noronha, Glass Onion Pictures

Cataloguing in Publication Data
Bowden, Rob
  Globalisation. - (21st century debates)
  1. Globalisation - Juvenile literature
  I. Title
  337

ISBN 0 7502 4241 8

Printed in Hong Kong by Wing King Tong.

Hodder Children's Books, a division of Hodder Headline Limited, 338 Euston Road, London NW1 3BH

Picture acknowledgements: Corbis 36 (Julia Waterlow/Eye Ubiquitous); James Davis Travel Photography 37; EASI-Images 5, 11, 22, 32, 38 and 57 (Rob Bowden); Eye Ubiquitous 14 (P. Thompson), 15, 20 (Stephen Rafferty), 25 (James Mollison), 27, 40 (L. Fordyce), 49, 58 (Jonathan Prangnell); Popperfoto 4 (NASA), 6 (Erik de Castro), 8, 9, 17, 18, 23 (Lee Jae-Won), 26 (Ira Schwarz), 31 (Madhu Kumar), 33 (Rafiqur Rahman), 34, 39 (Apichart Weerawong), 44, 46 (Juda Ngwenya), 47 (Jason Reed), 52 (Robert Sorbo), 53, 54, 59; Topham 42, 55 (C.W. McKeen); WTPix 7, 12, 13, 16, 24 (Dana Smillie), 28, 29, 41, 43, 45, 50, 51.

Cover: Advertising in China demonstrates the global reach of big businesses.

CONTENTS

GLOBALISATION: WHAT DOES IT MEAN?

'For some, globalisation has been an instrument for progress. It has created wealth, expanded opportunities and provided a nurturing environment for ... enterprise. But for others, it has exacerbated [made worse] inequalities and insecurity. They fear that the risks are too great, the benefits too small'
Juan Somavia, Director-General, International Labour Organization (ILO)

Making sense of globalisation

At the start of the twenty-first century there is one issue that is discussed more than almost any other. That issue is globalisation. Hardly a day goes by without globalisation being mentioned by politicians, broadcasters and newspapers. It has made its way into schools, colleges and universities too. It can even be heard in discussions among the general public in the street, in shops or at work. It seems almost anything that happens today can be attributed to, or blamed upon, globalisation.

The Earth as seen from space. Twenty-first century communications and technology make our planet seem ever smaller.

But what exactly is globalisation? In fact, relatively few people would be able to give a clear answer. This is not surprising, as even the experts cannot agree on what globalisation means. It is a very complicated issue, with many different sides, but it cannot be ignored. Making sense of globalisation should be a priority for anyone concerned about the future well-being of the human race and our planet.

New world or new word?

One of the central debates concerning globalisation is the use of the word itself. Many people, including most politicians, use 'globalisation' to describe the changing nature of the world around us as we move further into the twenty-first century. It is used to explain changes in world politics, in the global economy, in trade and industry, in crime and terrorism, in environmental threats and solutions, and even in social attitudes and behaviour.

FACT

The word globalisation is now so widely used that a typical Internet search engine will give you over two million results!

The UK, like many countries, is becoming an increasingly multicultural society in an era of globalisation. Multicultural street carnivals, like this one in Stoke-on-Trent in the Midlands, are now held in many English towns and cities. In the US, similar parades take place in cities like New York and Chicago.

Others take a more critical view of globalisation and say that it does not describe or explain a new world at all. To them, it is simply a new 'buzzword' for patterns and processes, such as colonization, migration and international trade, that have been happening for decades, or even centuries. By labelling these as 'globalisation', they argue that people are ignoring the past and the lessons it has taught us.

VIEWPOINT

'One can be sure that virtually every one of the 2,822 academic papers on globalisation written in 1998 included its own definition [of globalisation], as would each of the 589 new books on the subject published in that year.'
The Globalisation Guide 2002. Australian Apec Study Centre

VIEWPOINT

'Globalisation is not new, but the present era has distinctive features. Shrinking space, shrinking time and disappearing borders are linking people's lives more deeply, more intensely, more immediately than ever before.'
United Nations Human Development Report, 1999

VIEWPOINT

'Today, every part of the natural and human world is linked to every other. Local decisions have a global impact.'
United Nations Population Fund (UNFPA), 'The State of the World's Population', 2001

Two Chinese office workers surf the Internet at a cybercafé in Beijing.

Defining the indefinable?

With so many differing views on globalisation, defining the term is a very difficult task. However there are some common features of most definitions, which are worth considering at the outset. We will look at each of them in more detail in later chapters.

- Interdependency – the idea that people around the world are increasingly dependent on one another. What happens in one place has an effect on people elsewhere.
- Interconnection – the idea that we are connected to people and places that were previously distant and unknown.
- Shrinking of space – the idea that distances are less important. Far-off places are now within easy reach.
- Speeding up of time – the idea that the world is operating at an ever faster pace. News, money, ideas, information and people are moving around with increasing speed.
- Technology – the idea that technological developments, such as jet aircraft, telephones, the Internet, satellite television, etc, make globalisation possible.
- Capital – the idea that it is the flow of money and investments around the world that drives the globalisation process.

The world we're in

Whether we choose to use the word or not, we live in a world where globalisation affects all of us. The clothes we wear, the food we eat, the television we watch, the holidays we take, the cars we travel in, the music we listen to, and the news we follow bring us into closer contact with previously distant people

weblinks

For an introduction to globalisation, go to www.waylinks.co.uk/ series/21debates/globalisation

and places. Although many of these encounters may pass unnoticed, anyone living in the world's more developed countries experiences some form of global interaction every single day. And in the less developed countries of the world, people's lives are increasingly shaped by global forces, many of them beyond the control of those living there.

This means that globalisation is a truly world-wide process. It directly affects you and, more importantly, is also affected by you. You have a role to play in shaping the future of the so-called global society. This book will help you in that role by introducing you to some of the most important ideas and arguments in the globalisation debate.

Global marketing ensures that some products are available all over the world, even in places like this small town in the Kenyan highlands in Africa.

DEBATE

Before you read on, think about the ways in which your life is affected by and affects globalisation. Try making a list to see how many come up in the rest of the book.

A FAST-MOVING WORLD

The switchboard at an international press agency in London in 1970. Many of the items, including the telephone system and the manual typewriter, are barely recognizable today.

Faster, faster, faster...

Speed is a central element of globalisation. All around us, the world seems to be moving at an ever-faster rate. The best example of this is the movement of information. In 1900 the first global communications network – the telegraph – was completed. This revolutionized the flow of information, cutting down the time it took for information and news to spread around the world. For example, the time it took to send information from London to New York, was reduced from ten days (by surface mail) to just two. Even more dramatically, a message sent from London to Sydney, which previously took seventy days to arrive, now took only four days. At the time people thought of this as virtually instant communication, like being in two places at once.

Today, the four days it took for information from London to reach Sydney seems like an eternity. Incredible advances in telecommunications and satellite technology mean that information (not only words, but sounds and sights too) can be sent around the world in seconds. Take the Sydney 2000 Olympics, for example, a world sporting event that was beamed live into the homes of millions of people as it happened. Imagine waiting four days to find out who had won the 100 metres sprint!

Maurice Greene, of the USA, winning the gold medal for the men's 100 metres in the Sydney 2000 Olympics.

Keeping up

The speed of international communications and information flows is getting faster too. Technological developments, particularly in the computer and telecommunications industries, are so rapid that keeping up can be a real problem. Computers bought only a few years ago can seem almost impossibly slow compared to the latest available models. People can now use their mobile phones to access the Internet or have news or sports results sent to them as the events happen. None of this was possible just a few years ago. Indeed it may have seemed like something from a science fiction movie as little as ten years ago.

It is this rapid development that makes globalisation possible. But it also raises serious concerns for those who are unable to keep up with the pace of change. What happens to those who are left out of the technological revolution? This is an issue of great concern to critics of globalisation.

Since 1970 the speed of microprocessors has doubled every eighteen months.

VIEWPOINT

'New transport, communication and information technologies intensify competition while allowing firms to spread and manage international operations more efficiently.'
United Nations Conference on Trade and Development (UNCTAD) World Investment Report. 2001

On the move

Some of the greatest technological developments of the past have been in transportation and this plays a vital role in globalisation. From the horse-drawn stagecoach to the train, from the car to the jet aircraft, human beings have constantly managed to shrink space by reducing journey times. In the mid-1930s, for example, a flight from London to Bangkok took eight days in an aircraft that could carry only eleven passengers. By 2002 this same journey could be done in just ten hours and in an aircraft carrying close to 400 people. Today, jet aircraft have made international travel easier and more affordable. Business leaders can fly to their factories, partners or clients in other cities or countries in just a few hours. This has helped production, labour forces and markets to become increasingly international. For example, managers based in the USA may have staff and factories in Europe or Asia, as well as (or instead of) their home country.

The jet aircraft has also caused a boom in travel for personal and leisure purposes. This can be most clearly measured by the growth in international tourism, an industry that many consider to be the clearest example of globalisation. In 1950 there were just 25 million international arrivals (people arriving in countries around the world). But by 2000 there were 698 million, and the figure is set to pass 1 billion by 2010.

Improved methods of transport also allow faster movement of goods around the world. For instance, Kenyan companies use air freight to fly fresh flowers to Europe every night. This is so efficient that the flowers can take as little as thirty-six hours to get from fields in Kenya to supermarket shelves in Europe. Without such improvements it would have been impossible for Kenyan flower farms to

CUSTOMER SPECIFICATION
DATE: 01-01-02
DAY: 01
WEEK: 01
ASDA-POSY MIX
CROP-Mix of Roses, Standard Carnation
and filler.

LENGTH - 40 CM

COLOUR- Yellow, Orange, Pink, White
and Bi-Colour.
- Colour should be co-ordinated
for both Roses and Standard
carnation Roses.
- Carnation
- Filler

Kenyan flowers being packed for export to Europe's supermarkets. Improved transport networks have helped to make such international trade possible.

compete in the European flower market, as their goods would have perished using more traditional transport such as ships.

Even transport by ship has speeded up, thanks to incredible engineering achievements such as the Suez Canal (connecting the Indian Ocean to the Mediterranean, and onwards to the Atlantic), and the Panama Canal (connecting the Atlantic and Pacific Oceans). By avoiding the need to sail around the continents of Africa and South America respectively, these canals reduced journey times dramatically and boosted international trade – another central element of globalisation.

weblinks

For more information on the Panama Canal, go to www.waylinks.co.uk/series/21debates/globalisation

VIEWPOINT

'The question we have to learn to ask about new technology is not whether it benefits us, but whom does it benefit most? For ... the electronic revolution has far more to offer the largest enterprises on the planet than it does to you and me'

Jerry Mander, President. International Forum on Globalisation (IFG)

The World-Wide Web?

The Internet is often seen as the ultimate symbol of globalisation. It allows us to communicate with people on the other side of the world, to do business with distant companies, and to share experiences with people we may never meet. It brings the world into our own schools, homes and offices. But is the Internet, also known as the 'world-wide web', really as global as we think? It certainly has plenty of users, with over 400 million by late 2000, from less than 20 million in late 1995. However, even if it reaches the expected 1 billion users by 2005, this is still less than 1 in 6 of the world's population.

What is more, most Internet use is concentrated in just a few key regions and countries of the world. Around 80 per cent of Internet users live in the more developed regions (including the USA, Japan, Australia and Europe) that are home to just 14 per cent of the world's population. The vast majority of the world's people play little or no part in this new technological revolution. This has led many to say that 'the world-wide web' is more like a series of

In some parts of the developing world, particularly the major cities, new telecommunications technology is reasonably established. This young Kenyan woman talks on her mobile phone in Nairobi, the Kenyan capital.

well-connected 'hubs', with the rest of the world simply passed by. In fact this makes the Internet highly appropriate as a symbol of globalisation because, time and time again, as you will see in this book, it is the same places that are included and excluded from other aspects of globalisation.

FACT

South Asia is home to 23 per cent of the world's population, but has just 1 per cent of its Internet users.

These signs advertise Internet and email services in India. Such services may be the only way that poorer communities can access global information networks.

Playing catch-up

Supporters of globalisation argue that communications technology will help poorer, less developed countries to 'catch up' with the more developed. It will provide them with new opportunities to sell their produce, attract overseas investors, and perhaps encourage international tourism. Critics are concerned, however, that the same technology also makes it easier for already wealthy economies to take advantage of the same opportunities. If this happens, then the benefits may only add to the wealth of the already wealthy and leave less developed regions still playing catch-up!

DEBATE

How important is technology to the process of globalisation? Is it possible for low-technology societies to compete in a new global era?

MONEY MATTERS

MONEY MATTERS

VIEWPOINTS

'Openness to
international market
forces and competition
[is] expected to allow
[developing] countries
to alter both the pace
and the pattern of
their participation in
international trade ...
to catch up with
industrial countries.'
*United Nations Conference
on Trade and Development
(UNCTAD) Trade and
Development Report, 2002*

'...trade in a more
deregulated
environment lowers the
income share of the
poor, whereas trade in
a more regulated
environment raises the
share of the poor.'
*Christian E. Weller and Adam
Hersh, The Long and Short
of It: Global Liberalization,
Poverty and Inequality,
Economic Policy Institute,
Washington DC, USA, 2002*

How much?

Globalisation is most often discussed in relation to the growth of international trade. Global trading activities have grown enormously over the past few decades partly because it has become so much easier to move capital (money) and goods from one country to another. Companies and investors can make decisions and transfer money or goods across the world almost at the touch of a button. And the volume of capital and goods being traded is almost unimaginably vast. In 1998, for example, some US$1.5 trillion of foreign currency was traded every day – equivalent to five times the annual income of sub-Saharan Africa!

The growth of international trade has been equally impressive, with merchandise (raw materials and manufactured goods) trade increasing twenty-fold between 1948 and 2000. The value of global

Traders at work at the Tokyo Stock Exchange, Japan. They can help to move billions of dollars worth of business around the world every day.

merchandise exports increased by more than 100 times over the same period, to reach US$6.19 trillion in 2000.

Open for business

We have seen that technological developments, such as the Internet and improved methods of transport, help make this possible, but there is another important factor. This is known as the 'opening-up' of economies to greater trade. Put simply, 'opening-up' means that governments remove barriers to international trade, making it easier for foreign companies to invest in and trade with their economies. Such barriers might include taxes, for example, or controls on labour or the environment. When these are removed, trade becomes freer and competition is encouraged.

The idea behind this so-called 'free-trade' system is to allow companies and individuals to choose more freely where to locate or conduct their business. While doing so, they are able to choose lower-cost opportunities and so maximize their profits. These higher profits can then be re-invested in further projects which in turn will lead to even greater profits, and so the cycle continues. Supporters of globalisation believe that, by encouraging economies to open-up for business, the free-trade system will create more jobs and lead to greater wealth for all. However, opponents of free trade argue that job insecurity and poverty have both increased because of free trade and that it is often the poorest who have been hardest hit.

A container ship at Rotterdam, in the Netherlands, one of the world's biggest ports. Containerization (transporting goods in standard containers) has helped to make global transport networks more compatible.

weblinks

For more information on trade and world poverty, go to
www.waylinks.co.uk/
series/21debates/globalisation

VIEWPOINT

'The geographical structure of FDI has become far more complex in recent years, a further indication of increased interconnectedness within the global economy.'
Peter Dicken, Global Shift: Transforming the World Economy, 1998

International hotspots

Critics of globalisation point out that trade and investment are usually limited to a few international hotspots. The easiest way to see this is by looking at the distribution of investments in trade and industry around the world, using a measure known as Foreign Direct Investment (or FDI for short).

Using FDI, we can see that the critics have a good point. Just three regions, the USA, the European Union and Japan, dominate FDI. Between 1998 and 2000, they accounted for 85 per cent of outgoing investment (outflows) and 75 per cent of incoming investment (inflows). What these figures show is that the majority of the world's FDI takes place within these three regions. This trend has led to them being called the 'global triad' ('triad' meaning three) and it is their dominance that concerns the critics. They argue that, as long as the triad continues to dominate international investment, less developed countries will find it very difficult to benefit.

A select few

Supporters of globalisation point out that, although still dominated by the global triad, the broader patterns of FDI are changing. For example, FDI in

An elegant pedestrian walkway in the city of Shanghai, China. China has benefited from inflows of FDI more than any other less developed country.

less developed countries has increased by over twelve times since 1980. However, this increase is unevenly shared and has benefited only a select few countries. Most notable among these is China, one of the world's most rapidly developing economies. Together with Hong Kong (which became part of China again in 1997), China has been the most favoured destination for FDI outside the global triad, since 1998. The main reasons for this include its good infrastructure (transport and communications), cheap and plentiful labour supply and low taxes.

FACT

In 2001, developing countries accounted for just 27.9 per cent of FDI, of which over a third went to China and Hong Kong alone.

This pot-holed road in Nairobi, Kenya, is an example of poor infrastructure which often discourages inward investment.

Other non-triad countries that attract significant amounts of FDI include several from Latin America and South-East Asia. Brazil, Mexico, Thailand and Singapore have been especially successful, but others such as Argentina, Malaysia and Indonesia are also popular with foreign investors. The countries of the Middle East and Africa attract relatively little FDI. In 2000, for example, Africa enjoyed only a 1 per cent share in global FDI.

Economic zones

Several countries have attempted to attract FDI and boost trade by setting up special economic zones. These are known as 'export processing zones' (EPZs) or sometimes as 'free-trade zones' (FTZs). By 2000 there were over 850 EPZs, distributed across seventy countries and employing 27 million people. An EPZ is an area in which foreign companies are invited to locate their factories and conduct their business. In return for their investment, the host government removes import or export tariffs (charges), and often allows companies to pay no taxes for a period of several years.

Bangladeshi women at work in a garment factory owned by Siam's Superior (HK) Ltd in the EPZ in the southern port city of Chittagong. About 27,000 Bangladeshis work in sixty-two export-only companies, of which thirty-seven are foreign-owned in this zone.

The hope is that, as companies become established in the EPZ, they will choose to make further investments. The EPZ is intended to act as a gateway for developing new skills and ideas in the host country. Not everyone believes that they really offer these so-called benefits however. In fact some critics feel that EPZs represent one of the worst sides of globalisation. They see them as parasites, taking what they need from the host economy for their own benefit, but giving little or nothing in return. The EPZ ends up as an enclave, isolated from the rest of the country. In the Philippines, for example, some EPZs are so protected behind barricades that even the local police are not allowed in!

Worse still, investors have no loyalty – they would quickly relocate their business to a competing EPZ if it offered them greater opportunities. In this way investors have been likened to tourists, moving between different resorts as it suits them best. Their ability to shop around for the best deals can even force governments to lower wages or other standards, such as health and safety or environmental regulations, in order to secure their investment.

False hopes?

So why do governments go to such lengths? They hope that, by opening their economies, creating EPZs and encouraging greater FDI, they can share in the wealth and prosperity promised by globalisation. But many see this as a false hope, suggesting that following such a path only allows the rich to become richer and makes the poor poorer still. Whatever the truth, it is clear that money matters a great deal and that the corporations who control this money have great power in a globalised world.

In 1998 China had 124 EPZs, employing an estimated 18 million people – more than in any other country.

In Sri Lanka's EPZs, investing companies are allowed to operate tax-free for ten years.

VIEWPOINT

'For the investors, free-trade zones are a sort of corporate Club-Med, where the hotel pays for everything and the guests live free, and where integration with the local culture and economy is kept to a bare minimum.'
Naomi Klein, No Logo, 2000

Do you think promoting free trade is a good way to help poorer nations play a greater role in the globalisation process?

CORPORATIONS –
THE GLOBAL GIANTS

Corporate kings!

In a globalised world the true rulers are the corporations. But these are not just ordinary corporations. These are enormous business empires, many with sales that are worth more than the economies of whole countries. In 1999, for example, General Motors' sales were higher than the national incomes (a measure known as Gross Domestic Product or GDP) of both Denmark and Norway and almost twenty-five times greater than the national income of Jamaica. On a broader scale, the ten largest global corporations had sales in 1999 of US$1,198 billion – more than the combined GDP of sub-Saharan Africa and South Asia (that are together home to a third of the world's population!). So, how have these corporations become so large and wealthy?

The key to their success is that they produce and sell their products and services internationally. Such corporations are known as Trans-National Corporations (TNCs) or sometimes Multi-National Corporations (MNCs). This simply means that they have operations (manufacturing plants, factories, offices, etc) in more than one country. Because they operate internationally, the influence of TNCs in international trade and finance grew rapidly during the last quarter of the twentieth century.

weblinks

For information on the world's 500 biggest corporations, go to www.waylinks.co.uk/series/21debates/globalisation

The entrance to a General Motors (GM) plant in Ontario, Canada. General Motors is today one of the world's biggest TNCs.

Today they account for an estimated two-thirds of world exports. They are also important to many of the world's leading economies, such as the USA (where US-based TNCs contribute over a quarter of America's GDP).

Comparative advantage

Globalisation allows TNCs to locate their operations wherever they can best maximize profits. If wages are lower in Asia than in the USA, for example, then a US-based TNC may choose to locate labour-intensive operations in Asia to reduce its wage costs. This type of decision-making by TNCs has given rise to new economic centres, such as Bangalore in India where several European and American TNCs have set up data processing, software development and customer support centres to benefit from lower labour costs. In Bangalore's 'silicon valley' an Indian graduate software developer may cost around US$3,700 per year, compared to US$60,000 for a US graduate offering the same skills in Silicon Valley, California. With global telecommunications making it so easy to do business over long distances, Bangalore clearly has a significant cost advantage.

VIEWPOINTS

'...get out of the way of big business and the free movements of trade and capital [by removing barriers], and every nation will be able to do what it does best'
New Scientist *magazine.*
April 2002

'...business itself is now the most powerful force for change in the world today, richer and faster by far than most governments. And what is it doing with this power? It is using free trade, the most powerful weapon at its disposal, to tighten its grip on the globe.'
Anita Roddick, founder of The Body Shop

Selected corporations compared with countries in 1999

Corporation or country	Sales or GDP (US$ billion)
General Motors	176.6
Denmark	176.0
Ford Motor Company	162.6
ExxonMobil Corporation	160.9
Wal-Mart Stores	137.6
South Africa	130.2
Israel	100.8
Malaysia	79.0
Sony Corporation	63.1
McDonald's Corporation	13.3
Jamaica	7.2

Sources: UNCTAD and World Bank

FACT

In 2001 there were over 60,000 TNCs, with most (around 50,000) based in Japan, the USA or the European Union.

A TNC located in Bangalore, with its low labour costs, clearly has a comparative advantage over its Californian competitors – it can produce the same service or product for less. The savings can be passed on to customers in the form of lower prices that, in turn, allow the company to gain a greater share of the market and further increase their power. The lower costs also mean the company can make greater profits, to be re-invested elsewhere.

Changing patterns of production

Comparative advantage has existed since the very beginnings of trade. The UK, for instance, traditionally had a comparative advantage in steel production because it had plentiful supplies of the raw materials – coal and iron ore – required to produce it. But globalisation has changed the nature of comparative advantage. For example, reductions of more than two-thirds in the cost of sea freight have reduced the importance of being located close to raw materials. It may now be cheaper to take the materials to a location where labour or land and rents cost less. As a result, traditional centres of comparative advantage have been in decline. In the UK, steel production declined from 28.3 million tonnes in 1970 to 17.2 million in 1995. Over the same period, steel

A derelict textile mill in Manchester, in the north of England. Many such industries have relocated their factories to other parts of the world in order to reduce their labour costs.

South Korea has developed a comparative advantage in shipbuilding due to locally available steel and lower labour costs. This Daewoo shipyard is the second biggest in the world.

production in South Korea, one of the new global centres, increased from 0.4 million to 36.7 million tonnes. Similar shifts can be seen in other industrial and manufacturing sectors, as TNCs take advantage of emerging centres of comparative advantage, created by globalisation.

Footloose?

TNCs are frequently accused of being 'footloose' because of their ability to relocate their operations as and when it suits them. Critics argue that this leaves countries and their workforces extremely vulnerable. In reality, many TNCs invest a lot of money in their global operations and will probably be reluctant to simply close them as a result of short-term problems or costs.

However, TNCs are increasingly starting to use contractors or sub-contractors for much of their production and in this situation things can be quite different. Contractors are normally local businesses. Though not owned by the TNC, they have an agreement (a contract) to produce goods for them.

The textile industry is largely organized around contracting systems. For example, in 2001 the clothing TNC Gap Inc. sourced its products from some 3,600 factories spread across fifty countries. The company itself owns none of the factories and so remains extremely 'footloose' (able to switch production from factory to factory and country to country as suits its needs). This flexibility is beneficial for the corporation, but can cause insecurity and hardship for those living in its producing nations.

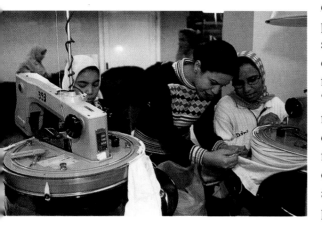

A clothing factory in Egypt, where labour costs are relatively low.

The footloose nature of TNCs also gives them significant power over governments who are keen to keep them in their countries. TNCs have, in the past, used these powers to influence government policies and decisions. In the Gambia, for example, government restrictions on tourism development were abolished following pressure from TNCs operating in the country's tourist industry. The Gambian government feared the loss of income if the tour operators decided to pull out of their country and so changed the law to keep them happy, despite the social and environmental dangers posed by excessive development.

Household names...

We are all very familiar with some TNCs, such as Coca-Cola. Having started to globalise in 1906 with its first bottling plants in Canada, Cuba and Panama, Coca-Cola now operates in nearly 200 countries around the world. They have been so successful that their products can be purchased in the most remote locations, from Andean mountain tops to Indonesian islands and even the Amazon rainforest! Other well-known TNCs include McDonald's, Nike, Ford, Wal-Mart, Sony, IBM,

weblinks

For more information about the Coca-Cola corporation, go to www.waylinks.co.uk/series/21debates/globalisation

Hewlett-Packard, and many more. In our daily lives we all come in to contact with the activities and products of hundreds of TNCs, whether we realize it or not.

Coca-Cola on sale in Arusha, Tanzania. Coca-Cola has become a truly global brand.

...and quiet giants

Many of the world's biggest TNCs operate as quiet giants, producing products and services that we use without really noticing. A good example of this is the Unilever Corporation. Unilever is based in the UK and the Netherlands and produces an enormous range of products sold throughout the world. The table below shows just a few of the company's many brands.

FACT

Unilever is one of the top twenty-five TNCs in the world, selling over forty brands in more than fifty countries. Its 1999 sales were US$44 billion.

Selected Unilever brands

Category	Brands
Frozen foods	Bird's Eye, Findus, Magnum
Dressings and spreads	Bertolli, Hellmann's, I Can't Believe It's Not Butter, Rama
Dietary products	Slimfast
Skincare	Ponds, Vaseline, Lux, Dove
Haircare	Organics, Sunsilk, Thermasilk
Deodorants	Axe (Lynx), Rexona (Sure), Impulse
Fragrance	House of Valentino, Calvin Klein
Household	Domestos, Cif

Source: Unilever website

News Corporation of Australia is another giant TNC. Although you may not have heard of it, you will probably be familiar with its products, such as the Sky and Fox television channels and the film company Twentieth Century Fox.

Strength and variety

Many of the giant TNCs have become powerful corporations by varying the products and services they provide. This is normally done by means of mergers and acquisitions. Mergers are when two companies join forces to create a stronger company or extend their operations into new countries. Exxon and Mobil, for example, both large oil TNCs in their own right, merged in 1999 to form ExxonMobil, the world's biggest oil company and second-largest of all TNCs.

Exxon and Mobil service stations sited next to each other in Falls Church, Virginia, USA. Once competitors, the two companies now operate together as the world's biggest oil company, ExxonMobil.

Acquisitions are when one company purchases another and incorporates it into its own business. For example, the Ford Motor Company purchased the British car manufacturer Jaguar in 1990 and the Swedish company Volvo in 1999. These acquisitions added different types of vehicle to those already being produced by Ford, giving the company greater strength and variety in the global vehicle industry.

ExxonMobil and Ford are both TNCs that focus on one particular product, but other TNCs have grown to include an incredible variety of different products and services. One of the most interesting of these is the French TNC Vivendi which, until relatively recently, was a water supply company in France. From 1980, Vivendi began to expand its water supply services into global markets. It also began diversifying into transport, waste management, construction and property. In 1983 it became involved in France's first pay-TV channel and so established a media and entertainment empire that today includes the Internet, publishing, satellite television, music, video and even theme parks. In barely twenty years, Vivendi has managed to diversify from selling water to become one of the world's largest TNCs.

'Jaws' on show at the Universal Studios theme park in Orlando, Florida, one of several theme parks owned by the French TNC Vivendi.

As TNCs continue to grow in strength, they are beginning to extend their control into new areas of our lives. For example, several TNCs are today involved in providing basic requirements such as water, electricity and health services. In the future they could also be involved in running schools, prisons and police forces.

DEBATE

Should we be concerned about the growing power of trans-national corporations? If so, why?

WINNERS AND LOSERS

VIEWPOINT

'Uneven globalisation is bringing not only integration, but also fragmentation – dividing communities, nations and regions into those that are integrated and those that are excluded.'
United Nations Development Programme (UNDP) Human Development Report, 1999

Many people in the developing world, like these children playing near a settlement in Kenya, lack the communications technology required to become part of the new global era.

For the global good?

Serious questions are currently being asked about the benefits of globalisation for all. As we have seen, certain countries and many TNCs have managed to use globalisation to accumulate great wealth and power. Others have not been so successful, however, and millions of people remain barely in touch with the new global era. For example, it is estimated that half the world's population has never made or received a telephone call. Without access to this very basic technology, how can such people and nations really be part of the global economy?

VIEWPOINT

'Companies have nothing against Africa, it's that the stability, infrastructure and skills are not there.'
Salim Jehar, Economist, United Nations Development Programme (UNDP)

A divided world

Critics of globalisation argue that, far from uniting the world, globalisation is actually making it more divided. And the evidence suggests that they may be right. In 1960, for example, the richest 20 per cent of the world's population controlled 70 per cent of global wealth. By 2000, their share of the world's wealth had increased to 88 per cent.

Within countries too, the gap between rich and poor continues to widen. For example, in the USA in 2002 just 1 per cent of households controlled 40 per cent of the nation's wealth – twice the wealth of 1970. Although this huge inequality may have been caused by many factors, globalisation has been blamed by some because of the way in which it favours the already wealthy and well-educated members of society.

Globalisation enables many of the wealthy people living in this expensive harbourside district of Sydney, Australia, to amass even more wealth.

Education is especially important in order to operate in the modern global economy. To use the Internet effectively, for instance, the ability to read English is almost essential, as it is the main language of nearly 80 per cent of the world's Internet sites. This is despite the fact that fewer than 1 in 10 people in the world speak English!

The poorest members of society are often denied a role in the global economy because they cannot read or write, or because they speak the wrong language. Wealthier people, in contrast, can generally afford to pay for their children to be educated to higher levels, so it is they who benefit the most from globalisation. Furthermore, many of the jobs formerly done by poorer sectors of society have been lost to foreign competition or replaced as companies invest in new machines to make their production processes more efficient.

VIEWPOINT

'In this new competitive world ... it is the unskilled that fare worst. They have become ... effectively commodities, easily replaceable by an ever-growing overseas supply'
Noreena Hertz, The Silent Takeover, 2001

VIEWPOINT

'More trade, more markets, more business, more information, more jobs, more opportunities. This is the promise of a globalised world'
UN Briefing Papers: Globalisation

weblinks

For more information about the world's richest people, go to www.waylinks.co.uk/series/21debates/globalisation

VIEWPOINT

'If you don't have educated people you don't have infrastructure, you don't have social organisation, nobody pays any attention to you, they never put factories there, they don't try to sell to you. You are on the globe but not in the global economy.'
Robert Reich, former US Labour Secretary

Personal gain

The most dramatic winners of globalisation are a small handful of chief executive officers (CEOs) of the world's largest TNCs and some of the investors who back them. They have made incredible personal gains as a result of globalisation. For example, Bill Gates, the CEO of Microsoft, had amassed a personal fortune worth US$52.8 billion by 2001, making him the world's richest person. This is equivalent to the combined national incomes of Kenya, Jamaica, Sudan, Nepal, Ecuador and Georgia. In fact, these select few people are so wealthy that the richest 200 of them share an income greater than that of the poorest 41 per cent of the world's population – about 2.4 billion people! If they were to donate just 1 per cent of their fortunes, these 200 people could fund primary education for all those currently out of school around the world. Some do use their fortunes to benefit those less fortunate than themselves. Bill Gates, for example, has a foundation that in 2001 gave out grants worth over US$1 billion to health and education projects around the world.

National losses

Just as some individuals make huge gains as a result of globalisation, thousands of others – indeed whole nations – suffer or lose out completely. Globally, there remain close to 3 billion people (nearly half the world's population) surviving on less than US$2 per day. These people have not shared in the wealth created by globalisation; they are not connected to the Internet; and the majority of them lack the education and skills necessary to play a role in the new global economy. Worse still, those that do have the skills are often attracted away from their home countries to work in those that already benefit the most.

This phenomenon has been called a 'brain drain' and it is another way in which many less developed countries are losing out. In India, for example, 100,000 professionals a year are expected to be granted visas by the United States to move there. It has been estimated that the loss of their skills will cost the Indian economy around US$2 billion. More importantly, it will remove many of the skills that could help India play a greater role in the global economy. For poor countries such losses are especially hard to bear, as they have often spent limited resources educating people to reach those standards.

A kerb-side school in Kolkata, India. Education is vital to joining the globalisation process.

FACT

In one year Nike paid the American basketball player Michael Jordan US$25 million to advertise its shoes – the same as 35,000 Vietnamese workers were paid to make them.

FACT

In 2002, it was
estimated that 3 per
cent of the world's
population lived outside
their country of origin.

New connections

One benefit of global labour markets is that, with
citizens working overseas, valuable trade and
business links can be established. In the UK, for
example, the Indian, Pakistani and Chinese
communities have developed strong trade links
with people in their countries of origin.

*This Chinese supermarket in
Manchester, in the north of
England, provides a taste of the
East in the West as well as serving
Manchester's Chinese community.*

Less developed countries can also benefit from
payments that overseas workers send home to their
families. These are known as remittances and can
make a significant contribution to the economy. In
Haiti, for example, they accounted for 17 per cent
of the national income in 2000, and over 10 per
cent in five other Latin American and Caribbean
(LAC) nations. In fact the LAC region received
over US$20 billion dollars in remittances in 2000,
making this form of income more important than
aid payments and equivalent to a third of FDI in
the region. As labour becomes increasingly
international due to globalisation, remittances will
become even more important to the economies
and development of less developed nations.

FACT

In 2000, overseas
workers from Latin
America and the
Caribbean made over
80 million remittance
payments.

Widening the gap

One of the most common criticisms of globalisation is that it is actually widening the gap between rich and poor. TNCs are often used as an example of this. By locating low-skilled, poorly paid employment in less developed regions, and keeping higher skilled and better-paid jobs in the more developed nations (where most TNCs are based), TNCs may be deepening the already significant divisions that exist in the world today. Some critics see this as exploitation, with wealthy countries becoming richer at the expense of the poor.

At the same time, wealthy nations have reduced the aid they are giving to poorer nations. This makes it harder for poorer nations to create conditions that will attract foreign investment and allow them to benefit from globalisation. The writing-off of debts is just one of the policies being suggested to help poorer economies compete more equally in the global economy. Many countries spend at least half their export earnings on paying debts back to wealthy nations. Such conditions make it difficult for them to invest in making their economies and workforce more global.

FACT

Africa spends US$14.5 billion each year repaying debts to the international community, but receives only US$12.7 billion in aid from other countries.

weblinks

For more information on campaigns aimed at solving Africa's debt problems, go to www.waylinks.co.uk/series/21debates/globalisation

Debt relief campaigners in Bangladesh mount a protest in 1999, calling for relief of foreign debts by 2000. The campaign for debt relief continues today.

Not all about money!

Though globalisation tends to be dominated by talk of business, finance and economics, it is about much more than just money. It is also about our daily lives and the ways in which we are all affected by the globalisation process. Just as with economic issues, there are winners and losers here too. The impact of globalisation on the environment is only one example.

As concern about the environment has increased in wealthy nations, many polluting activities have been relocated to countries where environmental standards are less strict. Poor countries are especially vulnerable to environmental pollution because their need for foreign income means that

A Bhopal victim, whose eyes were injured by the toxic gas, holds her child. There are many such innocent victims of globalisation, often in the world's poorest countries where they are least able to cope with such problems.

they often allow companies to operate with little care for the environment. Poor countries are also less able to monitor and treat the effects of any pollution. This can sometimes result in their populations suffering serious damage to their health. For example, in 1984 in Bhopal, India, poor standards in a US-owned Union Carbide chemical factory led to the accidental release of poisonous gas, killing more than 5,000 (according to official estimates) or possibly as many as 20,000 (who have died from gas-related illnesses, according to activists).

The digital divide

Globalisation also reveals clear winners and losers in the area of culture and especially the visual media of television and film. Many television programmes and films are today controlled by a handful of powerful TNCs. As well as making the programmes or films, they also often control their distribution and the ways in which we view them. This gives the TNCs great control over local cultures. In the UK, for example, live premiership football (the nation's main national sport) is now only available via satellite or cable television, which many families may find hard to afford.

The same is increasingly happening with digital TV viewing, leading to what some have called a 'digital divide'. As more and more television becomes available only on digital or satellite channels, a whole sector of society will be excluded from basic elements of their culture. Perhaps more importantly, an increasing amount of information or entertainment is only available on the Internet and therefore out of reach of those without access to computers. As the same process continues worldwide and is increasingly dominated by the same few corporations, so the digital divide, like the economic divide, is set to widen further.

weblinks

For more information on the digital divide, go to www.waylinks.co.uk/ series/21debates/globalisation

DEBATE

On balance, do you think globalisation is producing more winners or more losers? What could be done to make even more people winners?

A CULTURAL MELTING POT

A global village?

One idea that has received much attention in discussions about globalisation is the concept of 'a global village'. This is the idea that, as people around the world are brought into greater contact with one another, they are increasingly sharing the same social and cultural values and ideas. This has also been described as 'a cultural melting pot', with cultures from around the world adding to the pot, and a more uniform and shared culture emerging as a result.

There is certainly evidence to support this idea. In the Kenyan city of Nairobi, for example, young people enjoy the same styles of music and dress as those living in London or New York. Some elements of that same music and dress sense are actually based on African rhythms and styles that have spread into America and Europe.

The idea of a shared 'global culture' is strongest in the world's cities. For instance, a walk around the streets of Copenhagen, Denmark, or Vancouver, Canada, will reveal a similar blend of international restaurants, cafés, clothes shops and cinemas. Global culture

Staff at a branch of McDonald's in China. Such cultural symbols are today globally recognized.

extends well beyond major cities however. People living in the most remote places now appear to share social and cultural values with those on the other side of the world. But, in reality, how much sharing is there? Critics of globalisation argue that, rather than a genuine sharing of cultures, there is more of a one-way spread of Western (mainly North American and Western European) culture around the world. This is said to be closely linked with the dominance of TNCs, many of which are involved in cultural products such as food, fashion, music and film.

There is concern that, as the influence of Hollywood, MTV and McDonald's spreads around the world, local cultures will be eroded and the world will become more and more 'Americanized'. In this sense, cultures and traditions are said to be another loser of globalisation. In Mexico, for example, the once strong domestic film industry went from making over 100 films a year in the 1980s to fewer than ten films in 1998, as Hollywood took over.

The famous sign on the Hollywood hills in Los Angeles, centre of the global film industry.

VIEWPOINT

'I have seen villages in Africa that had vibrant culture and great communities that were disrupted and destroyed by the introduction of electricity [for powering radios and televisions]. I don't think a lot of electricity is a good thing. It is the fuel that powers a lot of multi-national imagery'
Gar Smith, Earth Island Institute, San Francisco, USA

The power of advertising

Advertising has played a major role in the spread of Western cultures around the world. Commercial breaks on television, the radio and in cinemas promote the latest products or trends to audiences of millions. Billboards and magazine adverts do the same in other areas of our lives. There is little escape from the advertisers' messages and often great pressure to be like other people by buying particular products or brands. Advertising is especially powerful because, unlike other aspects of globalisation such as the Internet or satellite television, it has the ability to reach and influence the whole of society, not just the wealthy.

Billboards, such as this one in Kenya advertising Fanta, reach a wide audience and can have a dramatic influence on local culture.

Young people are often specifically targeted by advertisers. Such targeting can have a strong influence on local cultures because many young people are easily influenced by the promotion of particular products and brands. In some societies, advertising has contributed to dramatic cultural shifts, such as changes in clothes or food, in the space of a single generation. In the remote West Pokot region of Kenya, for example, young people have largely abandoned traditional dress to wear Western clothes such as trousers, skirts and T-shirts.

Infinite choice

But are advertising and the influence of TNCs really responsible for the spread of a uniform culture? There are many who think not. Instead they would argue that globalisation has brought about more variety and difference than at any time in history. Far from being uniform, they say, there is now almost infinite cultural choice, and many influences come from outside Western culture. In the UK, for example, curry, an Indian dish, is the nation's favourite food. Meanwhile, throughout Europe and North America, cultural influences from the East, such as karate, yoga and sushi, have become increasingly integrated into everyday life. From this point of view, local cultures, far from being eroded, may actually be strengthened as they attract wider interest.

In some parts of the world, local cultures have also been strengthened by the growth of tourism – another result of globalisation. In fact it has been said that, without the interest of tourists, some cultures (such as the Masai of Kenya or the Padaung of Burma and Thailand) might be much weaker or could have disappeared altogether.

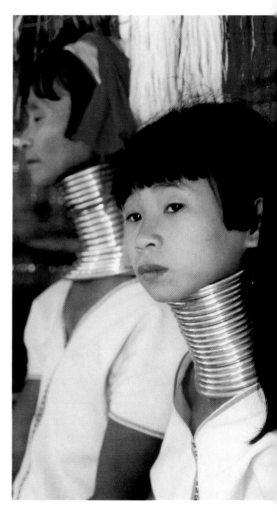

A twelve-year-old Padaung girl poses with her aunt at their village in northern Thailand. Tourists' interest in their culture has probably helped to preserve it, though some campaigners claim that the Padaung are being exploited.

Some commentators believe that, far from promoting cultural choice, globalisation can lead to exploitation of cultures. They argue that large TNCs turn cultures into commodities or tourist attractions and it is the TNCs who benefit, not the local people or their culture. Indeed, in many cases, the genuine culture seems to get lost as it is re-packaged into a more saleable product to suit the tourists and the TNCs promoting them. For example, in some locations ceremonies and dances have been reduced in length to suit the tight schedules of package tours.

Universal language

One noticeable result of globalisation has been the gradual disappearance of local languages, in favour of English. This is because many of the elements of globalisation (including international business, the media, the Internet and the travel industry) are heavily dominated by English. In some countries the ability to understand and speak English is

A Native American Indian, from the Ojibwa tribe, one of the many peoples whose languages are under threat.

considered essential for any involvement in the new global era. Young people, in particular, strive to learn English. In many parts of Africa, for instance, children communicate with each other in English while their parents continue to speak local languages. If such patterns continue in the coming generations then many local languages may well disappear – further victims of globalisation.

Some linguists (language scientists) believe that the loss of languages is an inevitable result of progress and that it is necessary for globalisation as it allows greater understanding and co-operation between different cultures. Others see the loss of languages as an example of powerful (and often wealthier) language groups forcing others to change. It is not just English that has this power however. In East Africa the Swahili language is rapidly replacing the many local languages of the region, and in China Mandarin has replaced many of the languages spoken by China's minority tribal communities.

FACT

Of the estimated 6,000 languages in the world, 23-30 per cent are no longer spoken by the current generation of children.

This road sign shows that the Irish Gaelic language is still alive. But for how much longer?

As we move into the opening decades of the twenty-first century, the state of the world's languages will give a good indication of the impact of globalisation on the world's cultures. If languages continue to decline, as predicted, the evidence will support those who believe that globalisation is leading to a more uniform global culture. If languages survive, however, then those who suggest that globalisation preserves and promotes cultural diversity may be proved right. Only time will tell.

DEBATE

Think about your own culture. How much of it is influenced by global forces and how much is still truly local?

THE GLOBAL ENVIRONMENT

The global commons

People may continue to debate whether culture is truly global, or how global the world economy is, but there is one issue that is definitely global – the environment. We all share the same planet and we all depend on its ability to support life. More importantly, we are dependent on one another's ability to manage and protect the environment for the benefit of all. This common dependence has led some commentators to refer to the environment as 'the global commons'.

A delicate balance

Mount Pinatubo erupts, in the Philippines, in 1991. Natural events such as this can have a global impact on the environment.

Nature provides clear examples of how environmental events in one area can have a much broader impact on the global commons. For example, in 1991 the eruption of Mount Pinatubo

in the Philippines threw so much ash and gas into the atmosphere that it created a cloud around the whole globe. This cloud blocked out some of the sun's energy and temporarily reduced average world temperatures by 0.5 to 1 degree Celsius. Earlier, in 1815, a similar eruption – of Tambora volcano in Indonesia – led to an even greater cooling. In fact 1816 was known in Europe and North America as 'the year without a summer', with both regions reporting frosts in the middle of their summer months.

The El Niño effect, caused by the occasional warming of the Pacific Ocean, is another example of a local event having a global impact. As the waters of the Pacific warm, they influence global rainfall and wind patterns with sometimes devastating effects. Normally well-watered areas can suffer drought and crop failures, while storms and flooding can plague areas that would not normally suffer such events.

Human interference

Volcanoes and El Niño provide strong reminders that we share the same global environment and we can all be affected by any changes in that environment. Increasingly, however, it is human activity, rather than nature's, that is doing the most harm. One of the most damaging results of human activity, especially our use of fossil fuels, is the emission of greenhouse gases (such as carbon dioxide and methane) into the atmosphere. These gases trap the heat of the planet and cause global warming. The warming of the Earth's atmosphere in turn influences weather patterns, sea levels and other elements of the environment.

Busy traffic in India. Vehicles are a major source of greenhouse gas emissions.

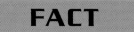

FACT

The ten warmest years
since atmospheric
records began in 1867
have all been since 1980.

Scientists have predicted that global warming will
lead to an increase in extreme weather events.
Glaciers will melt, making sea levels rise, leading to
the flooding of low-lying areas of land. The
distribution of wildlife could change and farming
could be severely disrupted as the conditions
required for growing particular crops are altered.
Recent events, such as the extreme flooding in
Europe during August 2002, and a long period of
drought in eastern and southern Africa, are already
considered by many to be proof of global warming.

*The famous Zwinger Museum of Art
in the German town of Dresden is
threatened by floods from the River
Elbe in August 2002. Volunteers
mounted a desperate battle to protect
the historic centre of Dresden.*

A number of environmentalists believe that
globalisation, with its emphasis on industry,
international trade and travel, is a major
contributor to global warming. It is certainly true
that emission levels have increased over the same
period that trade and industry have become more
global. In 2000, for example, emissions of carbon
dioxide (one of the most significant greenhouse
gases) were almost four times higher than in 1950.

Travel has also had a significant impact. Air travel, for example, already contributes over 3.5 per cent of all greenhouse gases. And, as travel by air becomes more frequent, this is expected to rise to about 14 per cent by 2050.

Cheaper air travel has led to more flights and increased emissions of greenhouse gases.

Waking up to reality

Globalisation is not all bad news for the environment however. It has also made people more aware of the environment and the dangers facing it. Greater media coverage, personal travel experiences and international co-operation have brought environmental issues into the homes of people far-removed from where they are actually happening. People are slowly beginning to understand that they are directly connected to, and influenced by, the state of the environment at both a local and global level.

Governments have also had to take environmental issues more seriously in recent years. New policies have been adopted by many countries to try to protect the environment better. And, globally, governments are working together in an attempt to tackle some of the biggest issues such as climate change. In 1997, for example, governments from 150 countries met in Kyoto, Japan, to discuss reductions in their emissions of greenhouse gases by the year 2012.

British deputy prime minister John Prescott (second left) arrives with delegates at the World Summit for Sustainable Development, in Johannesburg in 2002.

In August 2002, representatives from 184 nations demonstrated their commitment to global environmental issues by attending the World Summit on Sustainable Development in Johannesburg, South Africa. The summit was concerned with how to promote economic growth and rid the world of poverty, without causing further harm to the environment. Some see continued globalisation as an answer to this problem, but critics fear that globalisation will only create greater inequalities and lead to more environmental damage.

Playing fair

Environmentalists are especially concerned about the actions of some of the world's largest TNCs when it comes to the environment. As their countries of origin (mainly in more developed regions) introduce tighter controls to protect the environment, many of these corporations are simply relocating their operations to countries where environmental protection is less strict (normally in less developed countries). This means that globalisation is leading to a transfer of pollution and environmental degradation from richer to poorer nations.

The poor are least able to cope with the effects of such pollution as they are often already weak from hunger or poor-quality diets. Many cannot afford healthcare to treat themselves if they become sick, and their lack of education means they are often powerless to resist the actions of TNCs. To make

VIEWPOINT

'Only when people are rich enough to feed themselves do they begin to think about the effect of their actions on the world around them and on future generations'
Bjorn Lomborg. Danish environmentalist and author

matters worse, the poor do not even benefit from the activities of TNCs that produce the pollution. Many of the products are exported to markets in more developed countries. Over time this means that globalisation not only produces economic inequalities, but environmental inequalities too. Those living in wealthy nations enjoy cleaner environments and a continued high standard of living by shifting their pollution to distant locations.

The governments of poorer nations can find it hard to turn TNCs away even if they are aware of the environmental damage caused by their actions. This is because of the income and employment that TNCs can offer. Governments can face similar problems if they try to introduce new laws to help protect the environment and the health of their people. TNCs may simply decide to leave and set up in another country where standards are less strict.

In 1997, forest fires, caused by forest clearance for farming and industry, produced a toxic haze that affected the health of an estimated 70 million people across South-East Asia. Here, Indonesian schoolchildren are forced to wear face masks in their schoolyard.

VIEWPOINT

'Overall, our aspiration is to do no damage to people or to the natural environment, as we pursue our primary goal of creating wealth and supplying energy to meet the needs of the world.'
John Browne, Group Chief Executive, BP, 2002

weblinks

For more information on 'environment-friendly industry', go to www.waylinks.co.uk/series/21debates/globalisation

VIEWPOINT

'Sadly, we have not made much progress in realizing the grand vision contained in [UN] Agenda 21 and other international agreements'
Thabo Mbeki, South African President, at Earth Summit 2002

Because of the vulnerability of poorer nations, environmentalists argue that it is up to TNCs to play fair and not take advantage of the lower environmental standards found in some countries. As a result of such pressures, many large TNCs have now adopted codes of conduct to monitor their impact on the environment and local populations.

Others, such as the energy giant British Petroleum (BP), have gone further than monitoring and are actually pursuing environmental policies in the belief that the future growth of their business depends on showing greater environmental responsibility. In 2001, for example, BP succeeded in meeting a company target to improve energy efficiencies that in turn reduced greenhouse gas emissions to 10 per cent below their 1990 levels. This was achieved ahead of the 2010 target date and at no cost to the business. Environmental groups have praised BP for this effort. They say that it proves large TNCs can do more to protect the environment without harming their businesses.

Time for action

As concern about the state of the global environment grows stronger, many campaigners are asking for more immediate action to protect the global commons. They are concerned that there is too much talk and not enough actually being done. At the 1992 Earth Summit in Rio de Janeiro, Brazil, world leaders agreed on a plan of action for the environment called Agenda 21. However, despite much initial optimism, relatively little has been achieved since the Earth Summit and few of the goals that were set have been met. In fact, many experts believe the environment has actually deteriorated since 1992.

Following the Earth Summit, a local version of Agenda 21, with the catchphrase 'Think Global,

Pop   Milk   Water
Only these are recycled here!

Neighborhood Energy Consortium - 644-7678

Young Pacific islanders recycling plastics.

Act Local', was promoted. This was intended to encourage local governments, communities and individuals to take more direct action to protect the global commons. Although there are some examples of successful local Agenda 21 initiatives, many people feel powerless against the might of the large TNCs that increasingly control the world's environment. In many instances, their requests for change have been ignored or rejected, despite evidence that the environment continues to suffer as a result. In such situations people are often left with little choice but to try to resist globalisation.

DEBATE

Does the better awareness that globalisation gives us about the environment outweigh its negative effects? How might globalisation be used to improve the environment?

RESISTING GLOBALISATION

VIEWPOINTS

'What is the worth of representation if ... our politicians now jump to the commands of corporations rather than of their known citizens?'
Noreena Hertz. The Silent Takeover. 2001

'Is corporate rule inevitable? Only if the laws we choose to put into place allow it. Citizens have the right to change those laws whenever they choose to do so.'
David Korten. President. People-Centred Development Forum. USA

weblinks

For more information about the negative side of globalisation, go to
www.waylinks.co.uk/ series/21debates/globalisation

A rising tide

Since the mid-1990s, there has been a rising tide of concern about globalisation and in particular the role of TNCs. This concern has now become so strong that it has turned into a resistance movement, determined to make governments and TNCs redirect globalisation for the good of all. What makes this so-called 'anti-globalisation movement' especially interesting is that it is not made up of world experts (though it does include some) but of ordinary individuals like you and me.

An Australian anti-globalisation protester. Such protests are increasingly common on both a local and global scale.

Across the world, people have become frustrated at the way their lives are dominated by the actions of large corporations and at the seeming inability of governments to do anything about it. Many people have lost their homes and jobs as a result of globalisation, or watched their local environment being destroyed or polluted. Others are simply concerned by what they see happening in different parts of the world and believe that something should be done about it. Their motives are extremely varied but most of those involved in the anti-globalisation movement share some of the same concerns.

People, not business!

Strongest among those concerns is the belief that a successful global society should function in the interests of people, rather than in the interests of big business. Protesters argue that corporations are gaining too much power and that the world's poor are being ignored, as the already wealthy continue to benefit from the current world trading system.

Poor living conditions in India. Anti-globalisation campaigners want to see such communities benefit more from globalisation in the future.

In Europe and the USA, for example, a system of subsidies (payments from the government) allows farmers to produce artificially cheap food which is then sold to poorer nations. Local farmers in the poorer countries are unable to compete with such low prices and so find there is no market for their produce. Those same farmers also find that they are unable to sell their produce abroad because the more developed regions have set up trade barriers that limit imports to protect their own farmers. Protesters want to see these unfair trading systems scrapped so that all nations have greater opportunities to benefit from globalisation.

FACT

75 per cent of Americans believe business has gained too much power over many parts of their lives.

VIEWPOINT

'Anti-globalisation has piggy-backed on globalisation. The resources, infrastructure and technology of a globalising world have enabled ... the anti-globalisation movement.'
James Harding, Financial Times *newspaper, UK*

Taking to the streets

In many parts of the world people have now begun to take direct action against globalisation and its negative consequences. For instance, in the early 1990s the chemical TNC DuPont tried to relocate a hazardous nylon manufacturing plant from the USA to India. Under pressure from the USA, the Indian government gave DuPont land in a village community in Tamil Nadu to build their plant. The local government and people were not consulted however. On learning about the environmental hazards (such as air pollution and toxic waste) that the plant could bring to their community, people took to the streets in protest and some began occupying the land to reclaim it for themselves. The government was forced to back down and withdraw permission for the plant.

Tamil Nadu is a good example of an effective local protest, but globalisation is a powerful force and has the support of world governments and numerous international organizations such as the World Bank and the World Trade Organization (WTO). To make a real difference, the resistance had to become global and this is exactly what happened in 1999 at a meeting of the WTO in Seattle, USA. As ministers met to discuss new trading agreements that would give even more power to TNCs, people from around the world gathered in a mass protest against globalisation. The protesters (including over 700 organizations and up to 60,000 individuals)

Protesters block a street in downtown Seattle in 1999, preventing delegates from reaching the Convention Center where WTO meetings were to be held.

A banner unveiled during the Seattle protest, highlighting the issue of TNCs subjecting workers from poorer countries to low pay and hazardous conditions, in order to produce cheap goods for export to wealthier countries.

── **weblinks** ──

For more information on the WTO, go to
www.waylinks.co.uk/
series/21debates/globalisation

caused the meeting to be abandoned and, in doing so, introduced the world to a new kind of global protest movement.

Since the Seattle protests, nearly every major meeting of world leaders has attracted similar gatherings of people opposed to globalisation. Ironically, it is the tools of globalisation – the Internet, telecommunications and cheap international travel – that have enabled the numerous anti-globalisation movements to form their global coalition. Without these elements, it would be hard for them to co-ordinate such large protests. Critics have been quick to point this out and often accuse the anti-globalisation movement of having few ideas for an alternative or fairer system. So, what *are* their ideas?

VIEWPOINT

'I think [the protesters] have made an important contribution by making people aware of the flaws of the system. People on the street had an impact on public opinion and corporations which sell to the public responded to that.'
George Soros, founder, Quantum Group of Funds

A fair chance

Giving all nations a fair chance to compete in the global economy is one of the main aims of the anti-globalisation movement. In particular, protesters argue that the crippling debts many of these countries owe to wealthy nations should be forgiven so that they can redirect their money into developing their economies instead of making debt repayments.

Campaigners are also concerned that workers and producers should be paid fairly for their labour. In many less developed countries, TNCs pay poor wages that barely provide sufficient income for basic survival. An alternative system of fair trading, in which people are paid a fair and guaranteed amount for their labour or produce, has been developing rapidly since the early 1990s. For example, it is now possible for customers in wealthier countries to purchase fairly traded coffee, tea, chocolate and bananas – all products that are traditionally dominated by large TNCs. Fair trade products are identified by an international Fairtrade labelling scheme.

weblinks

For more information on the Fairtrade organization, go to
www.waylinks.co.uk/
series/21debates/globalisation

A Peruvian woman shows her coffee harvest in the jungle town of Alto Incariado in 2002. Coffee farmers there have joined up with a local coffee co-operative, selling coffee beans carrying the Fairtrade label.

Staying local

Another campaign supported by those resisting globalisation is the idea of 'localization'. This promotes a return to local markets and locally produced goods and services. Supporters believe that it would help create strong local economies, build new skills and reduce environmental impacts. Food is often used as an example of the potential benefits. At present, an increasing amount of food consumed in more developed nations is transported across great distances by the TNCs that dominate the food industry. An average American meal, for example, will have travelled some 2,400 kilometres before it reaches the table and in the UK this has been measured at up to 3,860 kilometres! The environmental impact of the transport and packaging involved is enormous, and it could all be avoided by a return to more locally produced food.

Tomatoes on sale at a farmers' market in Syracuse, New York, USA. Local markets avoid the need to transport food long distances, thus reducing our use of environmentally damaging fossil fuels.

Of course some products, including certain foods, would still have to be traded at an international level because they could not be produced locally. Supporters of localization recognize this and say they are not opposed to global trade. Rather, they would like to see trade limited to those goods that cannot be provided locally, and avoid the current situation where identical products criss-cross the globe purely, it seems, for the sake of profit. The only ones to benefit from this are the corporations that control the trade.

DEBATE

Could 'localization' really work as an alternative to globalisation? How would your lifestyle change if you tried to make it as local as possible?

THE FUTURE OF GLOBALISATION

VIEWPOINTS

'I remain convinced that globalisation can benefit humankind as a whole. But clearly, at the moment, millions of people – perhaps even the majority of the human race – are being denied those benefits. They are poor not because they have too much globalisation, but too little or none at all.'
Kofi Annan, UN Secretary-General

'There is little sign that the economic benefits of the global village will be evenly distributed. The income gap between the rich and poor has widened over the last 50 years. The technology gap has yawned wider still.'
Richard Buckley,
Understanding Global Issues:
The Global Village, 1998

weblinks

For more information on key globalisation issues, go to
www.waylinks.co.uk/
series/21debates/globalisation

A mixed blessing

In the opening decade of the twenty-first century, globalisation remains one of the world's most pressing debates, giving rise to a huge range of conflicting opinions and ideas, and raising far more questions than answers. If globalisation is so good and has created so much wealth, then why do nearly a billion people still live in poverty? If globalisation encourages efficiency and enterprise, why is technology known to be harmful (to people and the environment) still so widely used? If the divide between rich and poor is getting wider at both a global and a local level, then how can globalisation be said to bring benefits for all?

It is little wonder that globalisation has become such a complicated and confusing issue to most people. There are certainly those who have made up their minds, and have emerged as strong supporters or critics of globalisation, but the vast majority of people remain unsure of where they stand and even more uncertain about the future of globalisation.

An inevitable process?

Many people follow the view of world politicians – that globalisation is an inevitable process, that it is here to stay. They would argue that too many people around the world are now dependent on international trade and global links for it all to suddenly disappear. Many (especially those living in more developed nations) would not want to lose such benefits. They enjoy a higher standard of living than ever before, greater opportunities to travel, and more personal choice in what they eat, drink, wear and enjoy.

But if all this is an inevitable result of globalisation, why do the vast majority of the world's population living in less developed countries not enjoy the same benefits? For them, globalisation has often meant the loss of their livelihoods and the destruction of their environments. To make matters worse, many are now seeing their traditions, beliefs, even their languages, replaced by the cultures of those controlling globalisation. This is not the beneficial global society that globalisation promises, but is there anything that can be done to avoid it?

St Stephen's Shopping Centre, Dublin, Ireland, where no expense has been spared to fulfil consumers' desires.

A change for the better

Far from accepting globalisation as an inevitable process, an increasing number of people believe that something can and should be done about it. They point to the success of initiatives such as the fair trade movement as examples of how global business can be beneficial for producers, businesses and consumers alike. The proceeds of fair trade have paid for thousands of children to start attending school and for hundreds of communities to be given improved healthcare facilities.

Ecotourism is another global initiative that has bought benefits and led to the greater protection of some of the planet's most endangered environments.

An ecotourist visits mountain gorillas in the Democratic Republic of the Congo. Ecotourism is said by some to be a beneficial example of globalisation.

In Uganda, for example, ecotourists wishing to visit and learn about the endangered mountain gorillas pay enough each year to fund not just the management of the gorilla parks but several other wildlife parks too. These are just two examples of how globalisation can be used for the good of the world's poor and the environment.

Take it personally!

Despite such positive examples, critics of globalisation warn that there are still many reasons to be concerned for the future. For example, they warn that big businesses could soon be taking even greater control over our lives as they become involved in providing basic services such as water, healthcare and even education. If such essential human needs fall into the control of TNCs whose main concern is making a profit, then many experts believe it could be disastrous for the world's poorest people.

One of the biggest concerns, however, is the attitude of the general public when it comes to globalisation. Too many people believe they are powerless to make any difference to the way society and the economy are currently run. In fact some are so convinced of this that they do not even turn out to vote anymore. The truth, campaigners say, is very different. Without voters, a politician cannot be heard, and without customers a business has no income. They believe that if we all take globalisation personally then our actions can make a real difference. Only time will tell whether they are right. Meanwhile, the ideas in this book will at least help you to make an informed decision about where you stand on this vital twenty-first century debate.

VIEWPOINTS

'...exports could provide poor countries and producers with access to larger markets, creating opportunities for income, employment and investment'
Kevin Watkins. Senior Policy Adviser. Oxfam

'Why is it that people from the North [more developed countries] think exports benefit us? They are wrecking our environment and increasing inequality'
Sara Larrain. a Chilean environmentalist

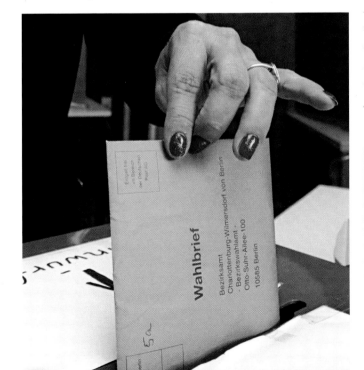

A woman votes in the German elections in 2002. By using their right to vote, ordinary people can make their views known to politicians and help influence whether globalisation becomes a force for good or ill in the world.

DEBATE

Having read this book, do you believe that globalisation can become a force for good in the future? What are the main obstacles to achieving this?

GLOSSARY

acquisition the act of taking over or buying something. In the business world, an acquisition refers to one company buying another in order to expand their business interests.

Chief Executive Officer (CEO) the person holding the most senior position in a company or corporation, who is responsible for the day-to-day management of the business.

coalition a union between two or more groups, normally made for political reasons.

Commonwealth of Independent States (CIS) a group of countries, now independent, that were once part of the former Soviet Union. They include Russia, the Ukraine and ten other countries.

comparative advantage circumstances allowing an individual, company or country to produce something for less than their competitors.

developed countries the wealthier countries of the world, including Europe, North America, Japan and Australia and New Zealand. People living there are normally healthy, well-educated and work in a wide variety of high-technology industries.

developing countries/less developed countries the poorer countries of the world, sometimes called the Third World and including most of Africa, Asia, Latin America and Oceania. People living there are often unhealthy, poorly educated and work in agriculture and low-technology industries.

diversify to become more varied. For example, a business may expand its operations into new areas, products or services.

ecotourism tourism that is sensitive to the impact on environments and local populations and seeks to benefit (or not harm) them by being there.

El Niño effect a warming of the oceans that causes changes in regional weather patterns, normally marked by extreme events such as droughts or floods.

emissions the release of waste products into the natural environment. These include car exhaust or aeroplane fumes into the air and waste water or sewage into streams or the sea.

enclave a small district or area that is distinctive from its surroundings. Enclaves can be environmental, economic, social or political in nature. For example, Export Processing Zones (EPZs) are often economic enclaves that exist within the wider economy of a country.

Export Processing Zone (EPZ) a special economic zone (sometimes also called a Free Trade Zone or FTZ) in which companies can conduct business with few or no barriers, such as tariffs on imports and exports.

Fairtrade products products for which producers are paid a fair (and often guaranteed) price. Coffee, tea, bananas and chocolate are among the Fairtrade products available in many supermarkets. The equivalent non-profit monitoring organization in the USA is TransFair USA.

Foreign Direct Investment (FDI) investments made by a company or organization based in one country into the economy of another. For example, a US shoe manufacturer might decide to invest in and open a factory in Thailand.

free trade international trade that is free from national or regional tariffs and/or regulations designed to limit imports and exports and protect local economies.

Free Trade Zone (FTZ) a special economic zone (sometimes also called an Export Processing Zone or EPZ) in which companies can conduct business with few or no barriers, such as tariffs on imports and exports.

global warming the gradual warming of the Earth's atmosphere as a result of greenhouse gases trapping heat. Human activity has increased the level of greenhouse gases, such as carbon dioxide and methane, in the atmosphere.

greenhouse gas an atmospheric gas that traps some of the heat radiating from the Earth's surface.

Gross Domestic Product (GDP) the monetary value of goods and services produced by a country in a single year; often measured per person (capita) as GDP per capita.

infrastructure networks that enable communication and/or people, transport and the economy to function. These networks include roads, railways, electricity and phone lines, and pipelines carrying oil or water.

Latin America and the Caribbean (LAC) a regional grouping often used when collecting data relating to trade and the economy.

localization a process by which economies become more local; the opposite of globalisation.

merger the process of two (or more) companies or organizations joining forces. In 1999, for example, the oil companies Exxon and Mobil merged to form ExxonMobil.

Multi-National Corporation (MNC) a business corporation that has offices, factories or other operations in several countries.

Organization for Economic Co-operation and Development (OECD) a group of mainly Western, developed nations that co-operate to promote economic growth and development.

tariff a tax, set by governments, which must be paid when goods are imported from another country.

Trans-National Corporation (TNC) a business corporation that has offices, factories or other operations in at least two, and often several, countries.

Western culture a set of cultural values, beliefs and interests originating mainly from North America and Western Europe.

BOOKS TO READ

Take It Personally
Anita Roddick
(Thorsons, 2001)

In the News: Globalisation
Iris Teichmann
(Franklin Watts, 2002)

21st Century Debates: Global Debt
Teresa Garlake
(Hodder Wayland, 2003)

Communications Close-Up: Global Networks
Ian S. Graham
(Raintree Steck-Vaughn Publishers, 2000)

The Dictionary of the Global Economy
Steve Bookbinder, Lynne Einleger, Peter Bell
(Editor)
(Franklin Watts, 2001)

Just the Facts: World Poverty
Rob Bowden
(Heinemann Library, 2002)

Globalisation – what's it all about?
Teachers In Development Education (TIDE)
(TIDE, 2001)

USEFUL ADDRESSES

World Trade Organization
Centre William Rappard
Rue de Lausanne 154
CH-1211 Geneva 21
Switzerland
Tel: 41 22 739 51 11

Oxfam
Oxfam House
274 Banbury Road
Oxford
OX2 7DZ
UK
Tel: 01865 312610

The Fairtrade Foundation
Suite 204
16 Baldwin's Gardens
London
EC1N 7RJ
UK
Tel: 0207 405 5942

TransFair USA
1611 Telegraph Avenue
Suite 900
Oakland
CA 94612
USA
Tel: 510 663 5260

Teachers In Development Education (TIDE)
Development Education Centre (DEC)
998 Bristol Road
Selly Oak
Birmingham
B29 6LE
UK
Tel: 0121 472 3255

Global Exchange
2017 Mission Street #303
San Francisco
California 94110
USA
Tel: 415 255 7296

INDEX

Numbers in **bold** refer to illustrations.